The One Minute Poster

Reproducible Posters and Flyers to Publicize Church Events

Concept by Patricia R. Dunmire

Illustrations by Chizuko Yasuda and Curt Dawson

Gospel Light

ISBN 0-8307-1442-1

How to make clean copies from this book.

You may make copies of portions of this book with a clean conscience if:

➤ you (or someone in your organization) are the original purchaser.

➤ you are using the copies you make for a noncommercial purpose (such as teaching or promoting a ministry) within your church or organization.

➤ You follow the instructions provided in this book.

However, it is _illegal_ for you to make copies if:

➤ you are using the material to promote, advertise or sell a product or service other than for ministry fundraising.

➤ you are using the material in or on a product for sale.

➤ you or your organization are **not** the original purchaser of this book.

By following these guidelines you help us keep our products affordable. Thank you.

Gospel Light

Contents

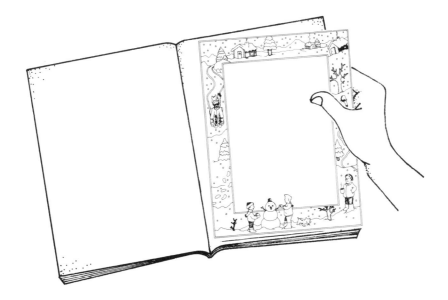

How to Use *The One Minute Poster*

Method A: Basic

1. Tear out the poster you want.

2. Reproduce one copy.

3. Fill in information.
   Make sure these questions are answered:
   What?
   Who?
   When?
   Where?

4. Reproduce as many copies as you need.
   Voila!

Method B: Get Crazy

Follow Steps 1-4 above, BUT:

➤ **Reduce or enlarge** to make bulletin inserts, program covers, newsletter blurbs, flyers or REALLY BIG posters! (A copy center can provide this service.)

To fit this size space: 4x5	**Reduce:** 50%
To fit this size space: 5x7	**Reduce:** 65%
To fit this size paper: 11x17	**Enlarge:** 130%
To fit this size paper: 8½x14	(Position extra space at top or bottom of poster. Use for extra information.)

➤ For *really* professional-looking posters, use **clip art** lettering (pp. 181, 183) or **transfer** letters and numbers (available at any art supply store).

➤ **Color** the art with felt pens. (For BIG jobs, enlist a Sunday School class or a senior citizen volunteer!)

➤ Make **re-usable** posters:

1. Reproduce posters WITHOUT added information.

2. Color, if desired.

3. Laminate or cover with clear adhesive-backed paper.

4. Write specific information with washable transparency pens.

Bible Study/Speaker

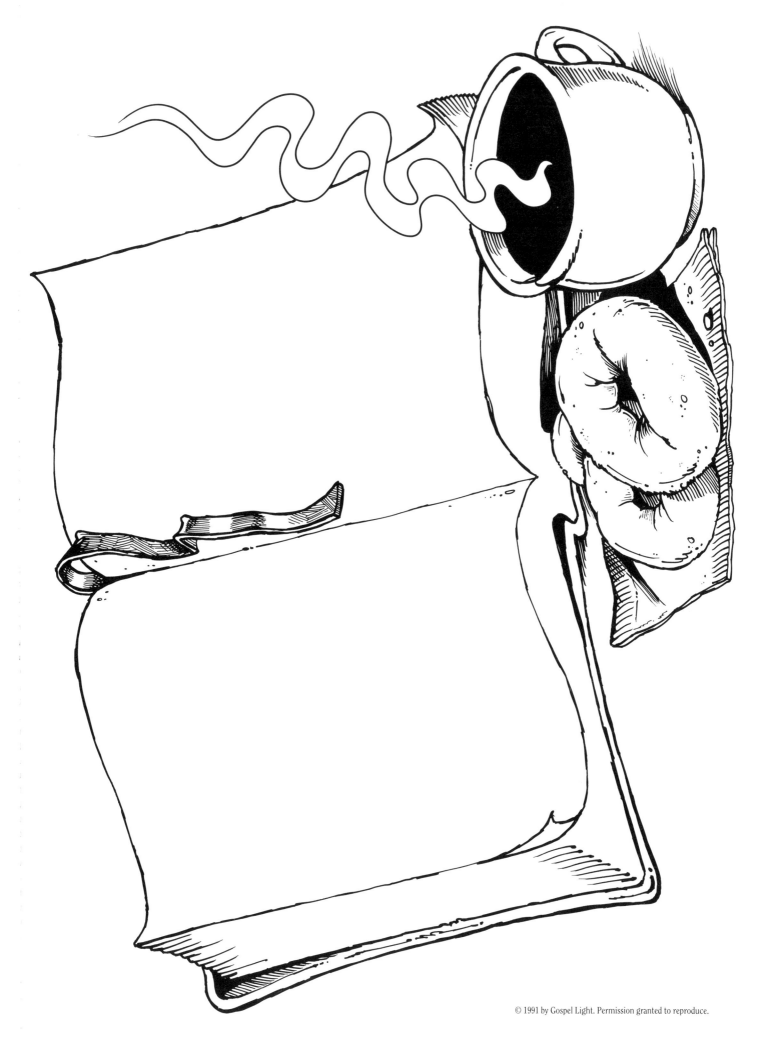

PSALM 104

¹Praise the LORD, O my soul. O LORD my God, you are very great; you are clothed with splendor and majesty.

²He wraps himself in light as with a garment; he stretches out the heavens like a tent

³and lays the
their water
and rides o

⁴He makes wi
his servant

⁵He set the ea
be moved.

⁶You covered
the waters

⁷But at your
of your th

⁸they flowed
into the v
them.

⁹You set a
again will

¹⁰He makes
flows bet

¹¹They give
wild don

¹²The birds
among th

¹³He waters
the earth

¹⁴He makes
for man
the eart

¹⁵wine that
his fac
heart.

¹⁶The tre
cedars

¹⁷There th
its hom

¹⁸The high mountains
crags are a refuge for the coneys.

¹⁹The moon marks off the seasons, and the sun knows when to go down.

²⁰You bring darkness, it becomes night, and all the beasts of the forest prowl.

²¹The lions roar for their prey and seek their food from God.

²²The sun rises, and they steal away; they return and lie down in their dens.

²³Then man goes out to his work, to his labor until evening.

²⁴How many are your works, O LORD! In wisdom you made them all; the earth is full of your

, teeming
ng things

and the
there.

eir food at

her it up;
re satisfied

e terrified;
hey die and

re created,

rever; may

embles, who
noke.

; I will sing

to him, as I

arth and the
LORD, O my

s name; make
e has done.

tell of all his

earts of those

⁴Look to the LORD and his strength; seek his face always.

⁵Remember the wonders he has done, his miracles, and the judgments he pronounced,

⁶O descendants of Abraham his servant, O sons of Jacob, his chosen ones.

⁷He is the LORD our God; his judgments are in all

Bible Study

Here's the Program

GUEST SPEAKER

Tools to Help You Grow...

When:

Where:

Camp

WHERE:

WHEN:

AGES:

Let's all go to...

CAMP

Where:

When:

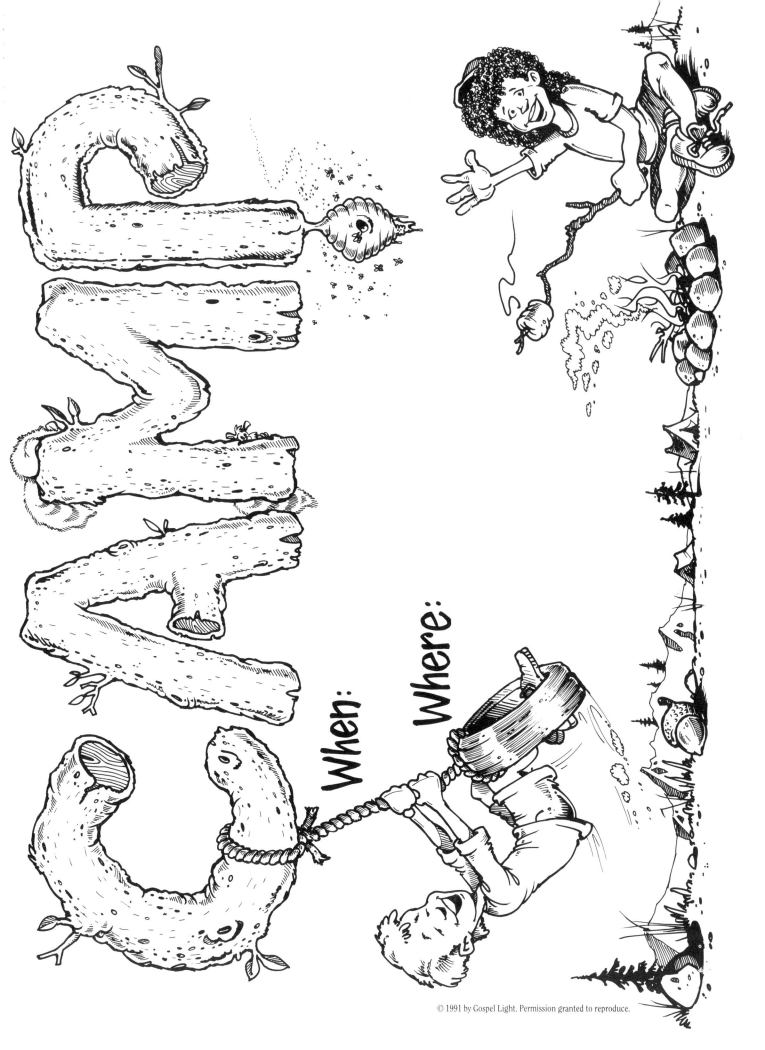

When:

Where:

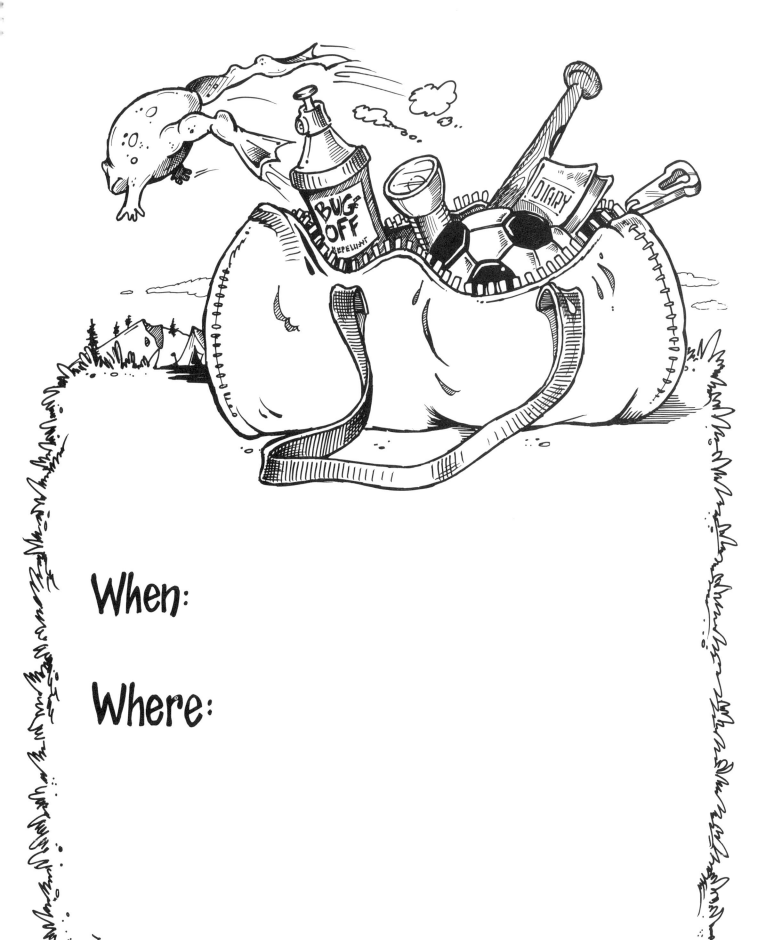

When:

Where:

Children/Youth

Bring a Friend!

Hey, Kids!

WHEN

WHAT

WHERE

COME ALONG!

Follow Us

When:

Where:

Here's Something Worth a...
CLOSER LOOK!

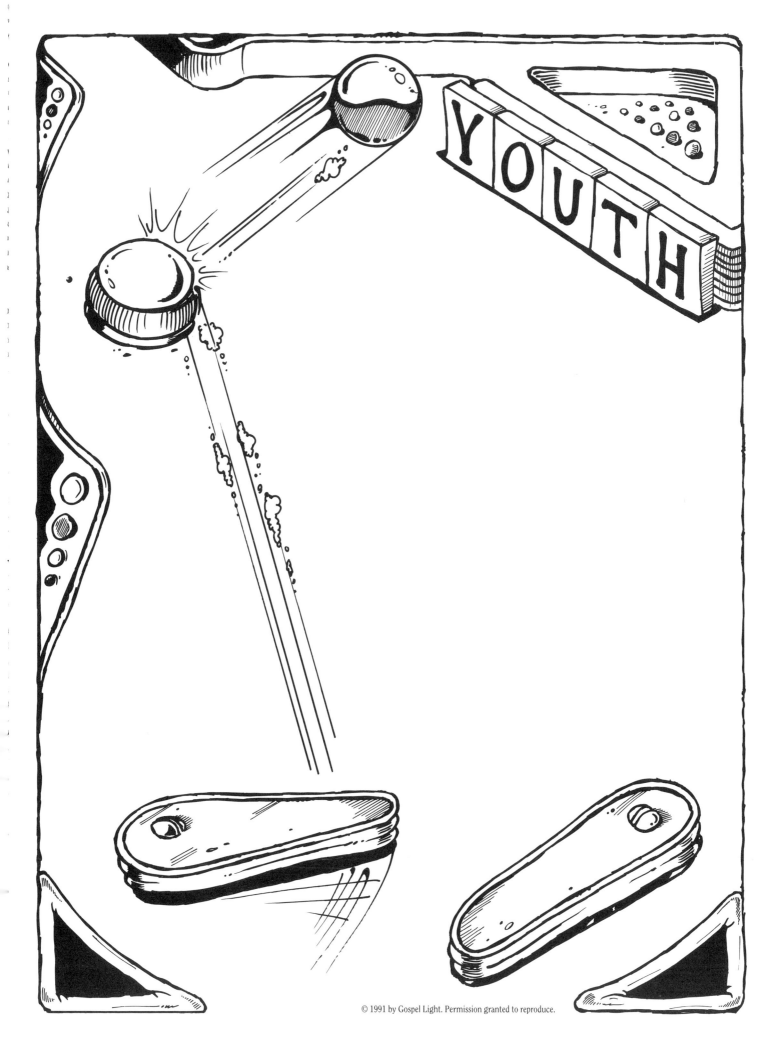

Sneak On Over...

when:

where:

When:

Where:

Here's Some Good Nose!

BE A PART OF THE Action

TAKE A LOOK!

When:

Where:

Food

When:

Where:

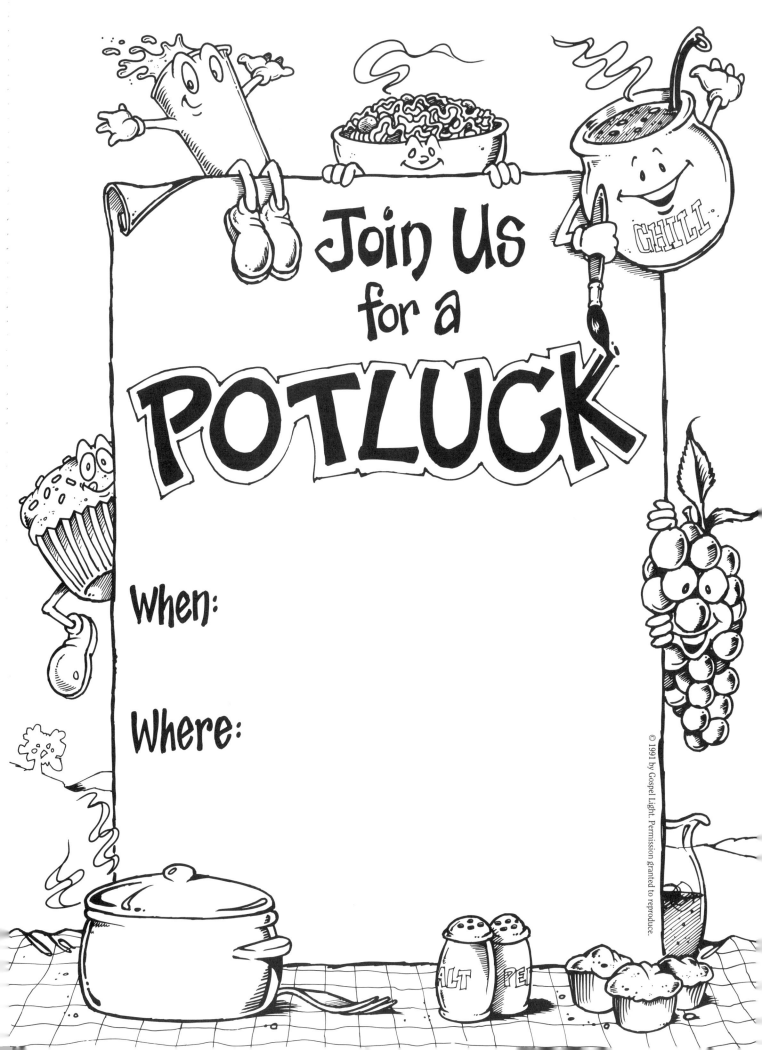

Join Us for a
POTLUCK

When:

Where:

You are invited

Come and dine

Missions/Fund-raiser

Where:

When:

MissionS

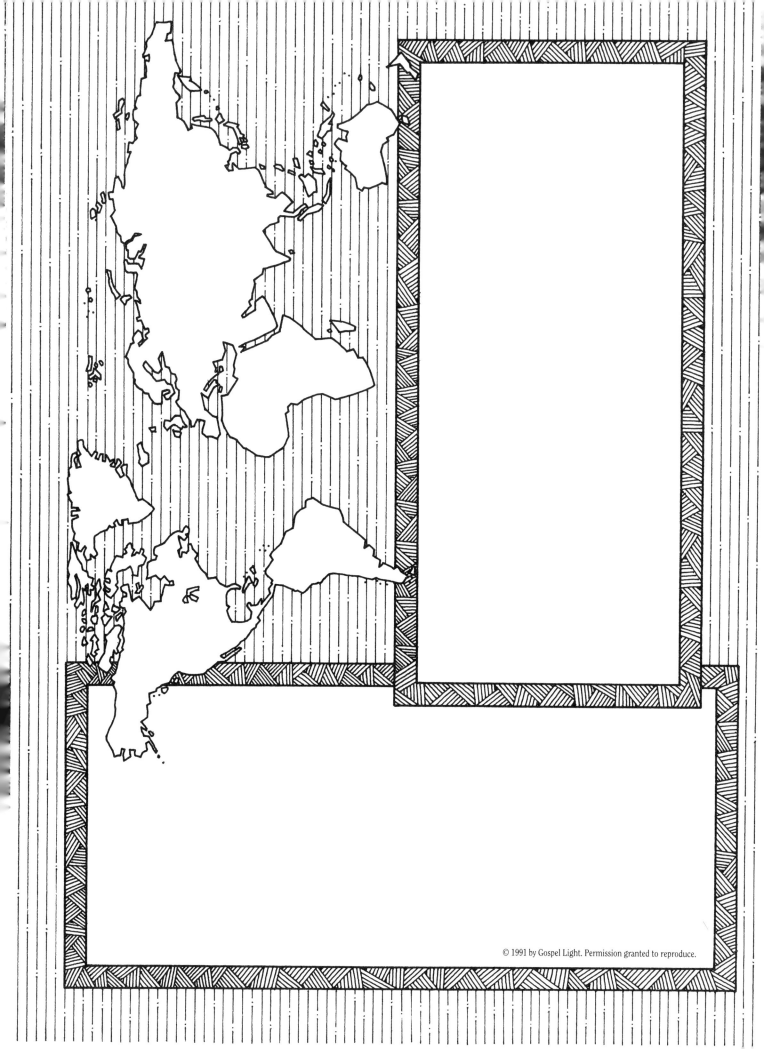

Reach Out

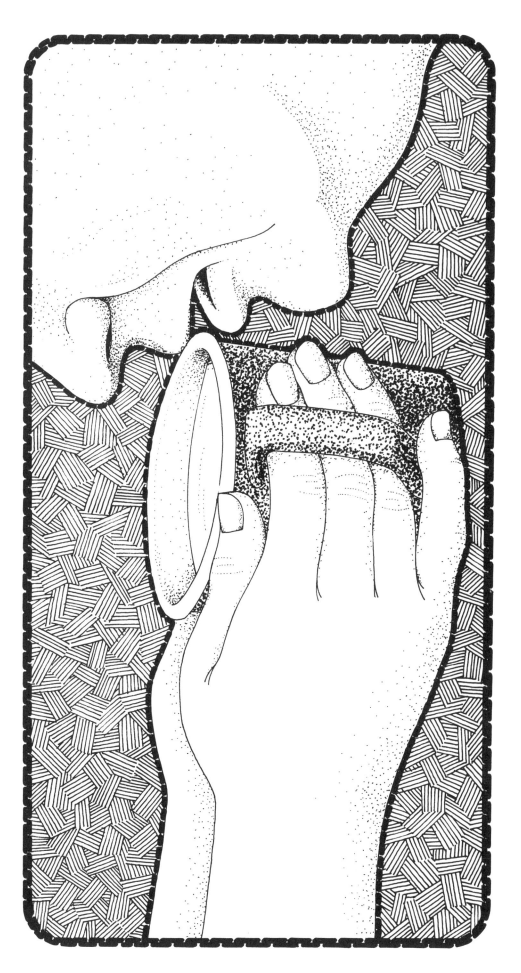

FUND-RAISER

We need your
HELPING
HANDS

Music

Special
Music

Where:

When:

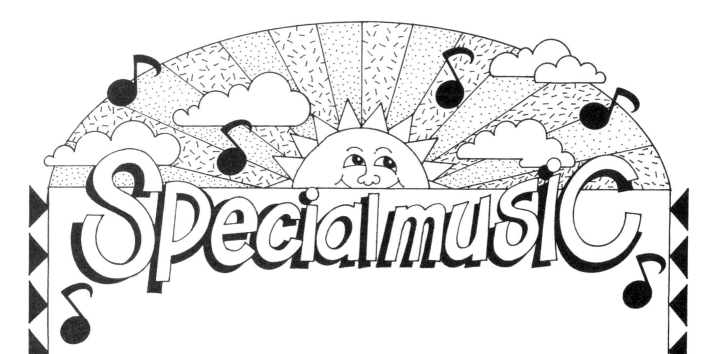

When:

Where:

Seasonal

Glad
Tidings

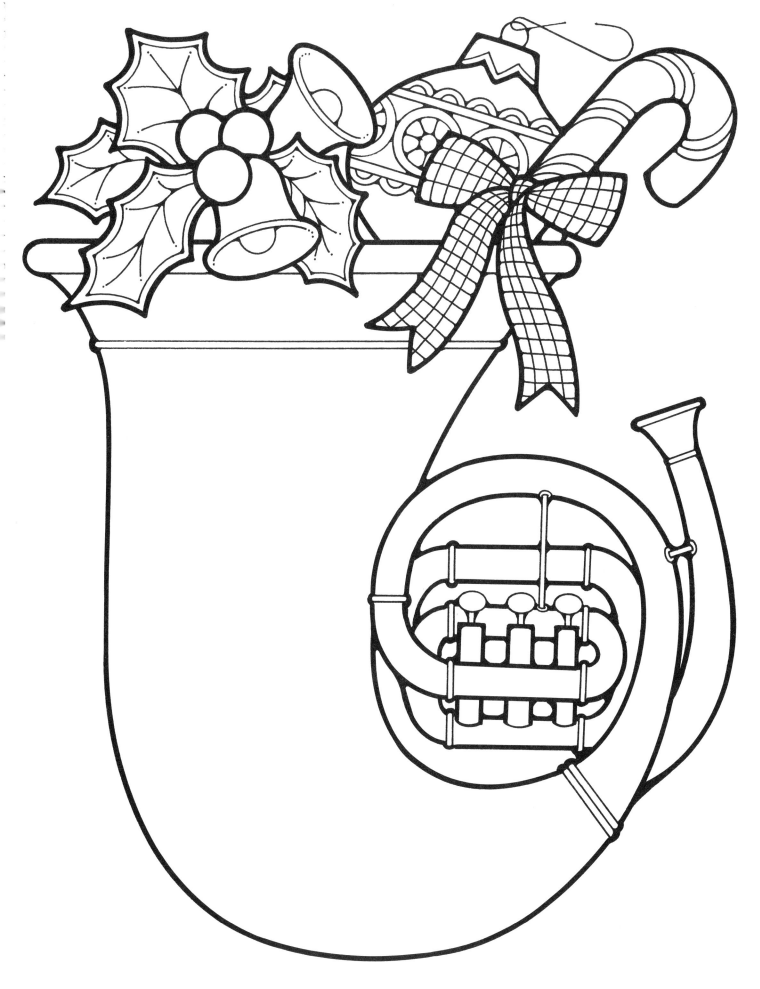

When:

Where:

Be Glad and Rejoice

LET THE EARTH REJOICE

REJOICE!

Warm up with some
Good News!

A LITTLE BIRD TOLD ME...

Wooden shoe like to come?

When:

Where:

Up and Away

Help!

General

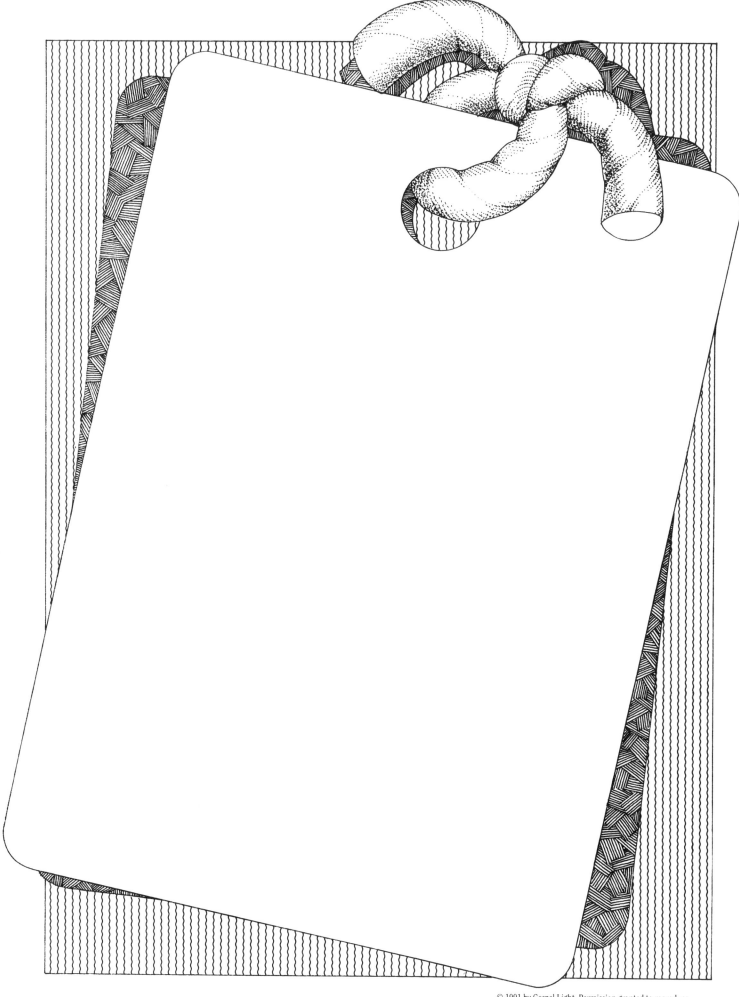

From the Heart

Food for Thought

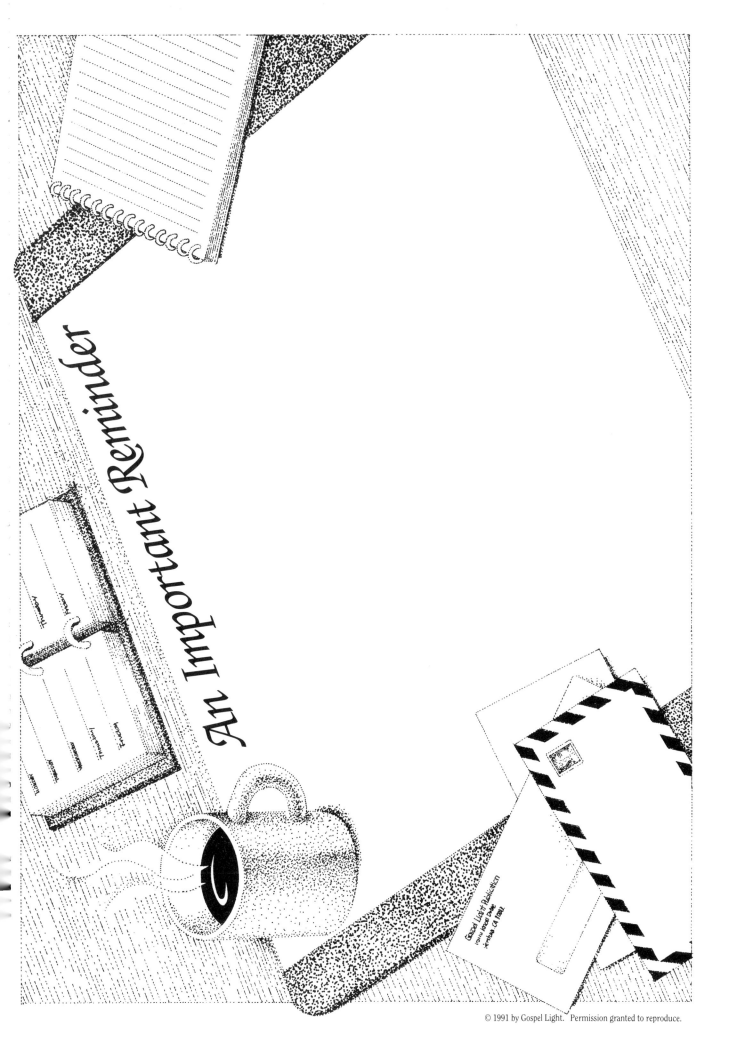

An Important Reminder

Kitty Letter

Points to Ponder

everyone is going to...

Announcement BARBECUE Movie Night

Bike Hike **Bible Study** Retreat

Backyard Bible School *Banquet*

Brunch **Budget** CAMP OUT Choir

Celebrate! *Concert* LUNCHEON

Choir Announcement *Easter* *Give Blood*

Christmas Program COMING UP...

Church Dinner Church Workday

Come and Sing CONGRATULATIONS!

DONATIONS Dates to Remember

Don't Forget Family Fun PICNIC

Guest Speaker Help Needed

REJOICE! **Hey, Kids!** *Harvest Happenings*

Calendar of Events **Bible Study**

Dates to Remember **Happy Thanksgiving**

Christmas Program Celebrate!

Have You Heard? **Seminar** Potluck

Important Message *Ladies' Bible Study*

Workday Let's Get Together

Missions **Mark It on Your Calendar**

Men's Bible Study **News of Note:**

MERRY CHRISTMAS **Men's Retreat**

Now Hear This! **Nursery News**

Youth News **Sign Up Now**

Special Concert Special Event

Sing Hallelujah! Special Music

Sweetheart Banquet Winter Camp

Teacher Training *Women's Retreat*

Teachers' Meeting You Are Invited

Valentine's Day Vacation Bible School

Potluck **Men's Bible Study** **Special Event**

Men's Retreat Women's Retreat *Missions*

Sign-up Sheet

Event _____

Date _____ **Time** _____

	Your name:	Your phone:
1		
2		
3		
4		
5		
6		
7		
8		
9		
10		
11		
12		
13		
14		
15		

JULY

AUGUST

SEPTEMBER

OCTOBER

NOVEMBER

DECEMBER

JANUARY

FEBRUARY

March

April

MAY

JUNE

187

SUNDAY	MONDAY	TUESDAY	WEDNESDAY	THURSDAY	FRIDAY	SATURDAY

189

Other Clip Art Books from Gospel Light

THE YOUTH WORKER'S **CLIP ART BOOK** features an assortment of art, greeting cards, youth worker forms (medical release, attendance, prayer charts, etc.), short Christian stories to add spiritual punch to your mail outs, certificates of recognition and a whole bunch of other fun things!   **T5077**

THE YOUTH WORKER'S **SON OF CLIP ART BOOK!** features over 1,000 drawings, borders, headers, Bible games (crosswords, mazes, etc.), surveys and questionnaires and ideas to make great-looking mailers, overhead transparencies and handouts for your youth program.   **T5079**

THE YOUTH WORKER'S **I WAS A TEENAGE CLIP ART BOOK** features ready-to-go drawings, borders and ideas to make great-looking mail outs, youth letters, and posters.   **T5100**

THE SUNDAY SCHOOL CLIP ART BOOK (For Nursery through Six Grade) is an invaluable aid for putting together class worksheets, announcements to parents, and much more. Hundreds of illustrations, designs, borders and patterns, all ready and waiting for you to use.   **T5081**

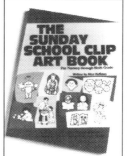 

THE **CHURCH BULLETIN CLIP ART BOOK** features over 1,000 illustrations, logos, borders, Scripture verses and designs to produce great-looking church bulletins, handbills, posters, overhead transparencies and Bible Study worksheets.   **T5083**

The Complete **BIBLE STORY CLIP ART BOOK** features art covering virtually every major Bible event in both the Old and New Testaments and includes maps, Bible clip art, diagrams, time lines and engravings.   **T5104**

THE **CHURCH MINISTRY CLIP ART BOOK** is a source for wonderful art, borders, Bible verses and more to spice up your ministry's Sunday bulletins, mail outs, handbills and posters.   **T5102**

You can obtain these truly helpful resources from your Christian supplier, or use the handy order blank below. To order by phone, call Gospel Light toll free 1-800-235-3415.

Please check the box of each book you wish to receive.

☐	1. THE YOUTH WORKER'S CLIP ART BOOK	T5077	$14.95
☐	2. THE YOUTH WORKER'S SON OF CLIP ART BOOK	T5079	$14.95
☐	3. I WAS A TEENAGE CLIP ART BOOK	T5100	$14.95
☐	4. THE SUNDAY SCHOOL CLIP ART BOOK	T5081	$14.95
☐	5. THE CHURCH BULLETIN CLIP ART BOOK	T5083	$14.95
☐	6. THE BIBLE STORY CLIP ART BOOK	T5104	$14.95
☐	7. THE CHURCH MINISTRY CLIP ART BOOK	T5102	$14.95

Mail this order form to:

CLIP ART
P.O. Box 3875
Ventura, CA 93003

☐ Please bill our church for cost plus shipping.

☐ I have enclosed a check for cost plus $2.00 shipping.

Your Name _____   Church Name _____

Church Address _____

City _____   State _____   Zip _____

Church Phone (   ) _____   Total Sunday School Size _____